Saying goodbye to...
A Parent

Chrysalis Children's Books

First published in the UK in 2003 by
Chrysalis Children's Books
An imprint of Chrysalis Books Group Plc
The Chrysalis Building
Bramley Road
London W10 6SP

Paperback edition first published in 2005

Text by Nicola Edwards

Editorial manager: Joyce Bentley
Senior editor: Sarah Nunn
Project editor: Jean Coppendale
Designer: Clare Sleven
Illustrations by: Sarah Roper
Picture researcher: Jenny Barlow
Consultant: Jenni Thomas, Chief Executive The
Child Bereavement Trust

ISBN 1 84138 833 5 (hb)
ISBN 1 84458 468 2 (pb)

British Library Cataloguing in Publication
Data for this book is available from the British
Library.

Printed in China

All reasonable efforts have been made to trace the relevant copyright holders of the images contained within
this book. If we were unable to reach you, please contact Chrysalis Children's Books.

Cover Bubbles/David Robinson 1 Bubbles/Frans-Rombout 4 Bubbles/David Robinson 5 Corbis/Ronnie
Kaufman 6 Bubbles/Lois Joy Thurston 7 Bubbles/Frans-Rombout 8 Bubbles/Chris Rout 9 Bubbles/Angela
Hampton 10 Corbis/George Shelley 11 Bubbles/Jennie Woodcock 12 Getty Images/Photodisc/SW
Productions 13 Getty Images/Ken Huang 14 Bubbles/Ian West 15 John Birdsall 16 Bubbles/Ian West 17
Corbis/Di Maggio/Kalish 18 Photofusion/Paul Baldesere 19 Getty Images/Photomundo 20 Getty
Images/Photodsic/Photomundo 21 Getty Images/Terry Vine 22, 23 and 24 Bubbles/Jennie Woodcock 25
Bubbles/Ian West 26 Bubbles/Peter Sylent 27 Bubbles/Loisjoy Thurston 28 Bubbles Frans-Rombout 29
Bubbles/Vicki Bonomo

Foreword

Confronting death and dying as an
adult is difficult but addressing these issues
with children is even harder. Children need
to hear the truth and sharing a book can
encourage and help both adults and
children to talk openly and honestly about
their feelings, something many of us find
difficult to do.

Written in a clear, sensitive and very caring
way, the **Saying Goodbye To...** series will
help parents, carers and teachers to meet
the needs of grieving children. Reading
about the variety of real life situations,
including the death of a pet, may enable
children to feel less alone and more able to
make sense of the bewildering emotions
and responses they feel when someone dies.

Being alongside grieving children is not
easy, the **Saying Goodbye To...** series
will help make this challenging task a little
less daunting.

Jenni Thomas OBE
Chief Executive
The Child Bereavement Trust

The Child Bereavement Trust
Registered Charity No. 04049

Contents

A mixture of feelings

When a parent dies, it can be terribly hard for a child to understand. **Bereaved** children often feel angry, that it is so unfair. They may feel lost and worried about the future. They may feel guilty, and keep wishing that they could have done something to stop their parent dying.

When Kelly's dad died, she felt angry with him for leaving her.

A child whose mum or dad has died needs **reassurance** that they did nothing to make the death happen. They need to know that they will always be cared for.

Jason needed to ask his dad lots of questions when his mum died.
His dad listened carefully and did his best to answer Jason's questions.
They talked to each other about how they were feeling.

Something to think about...
If you are **grieving** because your mum or dad has died,
it can help to share how you're feeling with someone you
trust who will understand.

Angry and sad

Being left without the parent who loved them so much can make children feel very unhappy and **lonely**. They may feel **jealous** of their friends whose parents are alive and well. They may even feel angry with their mum or dad for dying and leaving them.

Sonia felt sad that her mum wasn't there any more to say goodbye when she went to school.

Some children may feel embarrassed because now they have only one parent. This makes them feel that they are not like their friends any more.

Jack thought it was his fault when his dad died, because he'd sometimes been naughty. His mum hugged him and told him that nothing he had thought or done had caused his dad to die.

Afraid and confused

When a parent dies their child's world is turned upside-down. They may find it hard to believe that their mum or dad has died. They can feel as if life will never be normal again. Children often worry that their other parent will also die, and want to **protect** them. It can be a very frightening and unsettling time.

Samantha couldn't understand why her dad could die and leave her, and wondered why it had to happen to her.

David talked to his mum's friend when he felt sad. They both missed his mum a lot.

Something to do...

If you can, it's better to let someone know if you're feeling worried. If you don't feel like talking, write or draw about how you are feeling.

Feeling lonely and different

When a child's mum or dad dies, it can make them feel different from other children. Most children don't like being different. It makes them feel very lonely and sad. Some children feel like crying when they're sad. Crying can be a good way of letting out feelings of sadness. It can show others how they're feeling. But many children don't feel like crying. This doesn't mean they're not feeling just as sad.

Joe really missed his mum at his basketball tournament. But he was glad his dad was there to watch him play.

Edward's dad
promised him that
he would always
take care of him.

Something to think about...
Try not to keep your worries bottled up inside if you're
feeling afraid, lonely or confused. It can help people to be
sad together and **comfort** each other.

Asking questions

When a parent dies, it's natural for children to want to know what has happened to them. They'll want to ask lots of questions, perhaps over and over again. Sometimes adults try to protect children by not giving them honest information. But this can only make children more troubled and confused.

Jo told her mum she didn't understand why her dad had to die. Her mum said she didn't understand either, but that they could help each other when they felt sad.

Something to think about...
It helps children when adults talk to them about how they're feeling. Adults may be searching for answers to their own questions, too.

May's gran showed her photographs of her dad and told her stories about what he used to do when he was young.

What does death mean?

When a person dies, their body stops working and it cannot be repaired. It's the same as in nature when a plant or an animal dies. A dead body cannot feel anything, so there is no pain and no fear.

The dead person's body is placed in a **coffin**. Then after a special service, it may be buried in the ground or taken to a **crematorium**.

Some children choose to see their parent's body because otherwise they would find it hard to believe their mum or dad had died. Others choose not to.

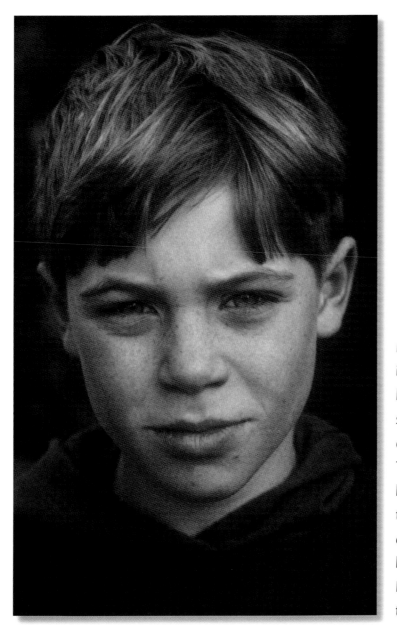

Mark's mum died in a **hospice**. It helped Mark to see his mum's body after she had died. The staff at the hospice were kind to Mark. They asked him how he was feeling. It helped Mark to talk to them.

15

Preparing for a funeral

A **funeral** is a special service where people can share their memories of the person who has died and say goodbye to them. It's important for children to know what will happen during a funeral. Then they can decide whether or not they want to be there. Some children find it comforting to be involved in the preparations for a funeral.

Nat helped to choose the flowers which were put on his mum's coffin.

Kate wrote a letter to say goodbye to her dad.

Something to think about...
Some children decide to go to their parent's funeral.
Others may decide just to go to the get-together after
the service – it's up to you.

At the funeral

There are different kinds of funeral service. Some are **religious**, others are not because different people have different beliefs. At a funeral, children can find it difficult to see the people they love looking so upset. It can also be a shock for some children to see the coffin being lowered into a **grave** or taken away to be cremated.

Adults and children praying together at the start of this **Buddhist** funeral service.

ut a funeral gives everyone a chance to remember the life of the person they knew and show they were important.

At this funeral the priest is asking people to remember the person who has died in their **prayers**.

Helping each other

When a child's mum or dad dies they can feel very alone, as if they are the only person it's ever happened to. Children often think that no one will be able to understand how they are feeling. But when someone dies they leave many people feeling sad, who can comfort each other. Adults often say that their children helped them when they were upset, by talking to them or just by being there with them.

The people who cared about Adam wanted to give him some happy times after his mum died.

It helped Samuel to talk to his friends after his dad died. They understood how Samuel was feeling.

Something to think about...
Sharing memories of the person who has died can be very comforting. You can talk to people about how they remember your mum or dad.

Holding on to memories

It's important for bereaved children to hold on to their memories of their mum or dad. Talking about them can help. So can looking at photos and watching videos of them. It's good to think about the things that made them who they were: how they looked, their favourite food, music and places, what they said and did, and all the things they helped their children to do. Some children say they know that their mummy or daddy will always be with them in their hearts.

Polly liked trying on her mum's favourite clothes. It helped her to think of her mum.

Something to think about...
Some children may decide to raise money for charity in memory of their mum or dad. You could go on a sponsored walk, do a sponsored swim or organise a bring and buy sale.

Looking through family photo albums helped Zoe and Patrick to remember their mum .

Understanding change

Although life will never be quite the same again, life does go on after a mum or dad has died. Family members can help each other to cope with any changes that have to happen. Slowly and gradually, children and their families adjust to their new lives, keeping all their memories of the parent who has died. Going through hard times together can make people in a family feel closer.

Grace and James liked having their friends round for tea.

Alice and Helen had fun on holiday
with their dad.

Difficult days

It's natural for children not to feel sad all the time when a parent dies. But it can be hard when something – perhaps a certain smell, a song or a television programme – reminds them of their mum or dad. They can suddenly feel very upset. On days like these, it can help children to think about their parent and remember how much they miss them.

Ben and Alex visited their dad's **grave** the year after he died, on his birthday. They brought some of their dad's favourite flowers to leave there.

26

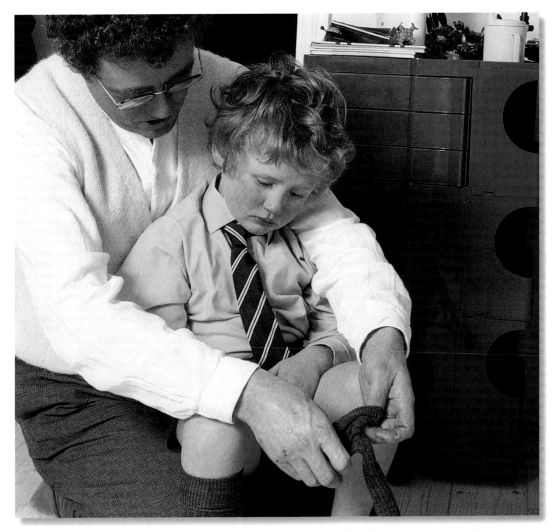

Tom felt sad on his first day at school. He wished his mum could see him in his new school uniform.

 **Something to do...**
Find ways of remembering your mum or dad that work best for you. Perhaps you could paint a picture, write a poem or plant some flowers.

Feeling happy again

Grieving for someone who has died is a natural thing to do. Everyone feels grief in their own way and takes the time they need to feel less upset. Gradually, children's happy memories of their parent become part of their thoughts, rather than making them feel sad. Their mum or dad will always be an important part of their lives and they'll never forget them.

Zak felt very happy when his mum told him how much he looked like his dad.

Charlotte would never forget the happy times when she'd played with her mum.

Something to think about...

Try not to feel **guilty** about enjoying yourself and not thinking about your mum or dad all the time – it's a normal part of grieving. Your parent loved you and wanted you to be happy.

Glossary

bereaved   being left behind when someone you love or care about dies

Buddhist   someone who follows the teachings of the Buddha, a great teacher who lived in India over 2000 years ago

coffin   the container in which a dead body is placed

comfort   to help someone who is sad to feel better

crematorium   a building to which dead bodies can be taken to be cremated, or burned

funeral   a special service in which people remember a person who has died and say goodbye to them

grave   a hole in the ground in which a coffin containing a dead body is buried

grieving   the natural feelings of sadness after someone has died

guilty   feeling bad, as if it's your fault that something is wrong

hospice   a building where people who are dying are looked after

jealous   wishing that what someone else has could be yours

lonely   feeling sad and alone

prayers   talking to God

protect   to take care of someone and keep them from harm

reassurance   the giving of comfort and help to someone who is feeling worried

religious   to do with a belief in God

trust   to feel that someone will not let you down

Useful addresses

The Child Bereavement Trust
A charity offering training, resources and support for professional carers and teachers working with bereaved children and grieving adults
Aston House
High Street
West Wycombe
Bucks HP14 3AG
Tel: 01494 446648
Information and Support Line: 0845 357 1000
E-mail: enquiries@childbereavement.org.uk
Website: www.childbereavement.org.uk
★ New interactive website where children and adults can send emails

Childhood Bereavement Network
An organization offering bereaved children and their families and caregivers information about the support services available to them.
Huntingdon House
278-290 Huntingdon Street
Nottingham NG1 3LY
Tel: 0115 911 8070
E-mail: cbn@ncb.org.uk
Website: www.ncb.org.uk/cbn

ChildLine
Childline's free, 24-hour helpline is staffed by trained counsellors, offering help and support to children and young people. The website includes information on bereavement.
Freepost 1111
London N1 0BR
Tel: 0800 11 11 (Freephone 24 hours)
Website: www.childline.org.uk

Cruse Bereavement Care
The Cruse helpline offers information and counselling to people of all ages who have been bereaved. The website offers additional information and support.

Cruse House
126 Sheen Road
Richmond
Surrey TW9 1UR
Tel: 020 8322 7227
Helpline: 0870 167 1677 (Mondays to Fridays 9.30am–5pm)
Website: www.crusebereavementcare.org.uk

The Samaritans
An organization offering support and help to anyone who is emotionally distressed.
Tel: 08457 90 90 90 (24 hours)
Website: www.samaritans.org.uk

Winston's Wish
A charity offering support and information to bereaved children and their families.
The Clara Burgess Centre
Gloucestershire Royal Hospital
Great Western Road
Gloucester GL1 3NN
Tel: 01452 394377
Family Line: 0845 20 30 40 5 (Mondays to Fridays 9.30am–5pm)
E-mail: info@winstonswish.org.uk
Website: www.winstonswish.org

Youth Access
An organization providing information about youth counselling services.
1-2 Taylors Yard
67 Alderbrook Road
London SW12 8AD
Tel: 020 8772 9900 (Monday to Fridays 9am–1pm, 2-5pm)
E-mail: admin@youthaccess.org.uk

Index